HOW TO CREATE THE FUTURE YOU WANT

GETTING FROM WHERE YOU ARE TO WHERE YOU OUGHT TO BE

by

Daniel Ayeni

Bloomington, IN  Milton Keynes, UK

 authorHOUSE®

AuthorHouse™
1663 Liberty Drive, Suite 200
Bloomington, IN 47403
www.authorhouse.com
Phone: 1-800-839-8640

AuthorHouse™ UK Ltd.
500 Avebury Boulevard
Central Milton Keynes, MK9 2BE
www.authorhouse.co.uk
Phone: 08001974150

First published by AuthorHouse 11/22/2006

ISBN: 978-1-4259-5724-7 (sc)

Printed in the United States of America
Bloomington, Indiana

This book is printed on acid-free paper.

Unless otherwise noted, Scripture quotations are from the HOLY BIBLE: KING JAMES VERSION

Scripture quotations noted The Message are from The Message: The New Testament in Contemporary English. Copyright © 1993 by Eugene H. Peterson.

Praise for
'How To Create The Future You Want'

"In my brief encounter with Daniel, I found him to possess a wonderful dedication to service and excellence, with the most infectious and impeccable attitude. This book 'How to create the future you want' is replete with deep nuggets of wisdom if you would take the time to investigate it; I am persuaded you will be glad you did. Look out for more from him in the future!

> Charles Khiran
>
> personal development trainer and
> motivational speaker

"By revealing personal testimonies, celebrity successes and failures as well as biblical examples, this book challenges the reader with some searching questions and gives insight to some key principles in creating a future for our lives. Ultimately placing an emphasis to believe and trust in God our Father".

> Deacon Julian Tobierre
>
> Business man, London

"I did enjoy this book. It made me think…about whom I am and where I want to be. I wasn't intending to think, but I did, and, as a result I am determined to be a bit more determined about the kind of future I want!"

> Pauline Banks, Wesley Owen Books and Music, London

"*How To Create The Future You Want* is an excellent book. Very positive! It would be a great book for anyone wanting to achieve the Impossible and change their mindset and focus to a positive one".

> Eula Clarke
> Vice Chairman
> Cultural & Diversity Network
> Barclays Bank

"This Book is a masterpiece, a must for every young person with dreams locked up inside them, and for the elderly wanting to re-fire".

Anthony Aisien
De Ultimate Generation, UK

"Amazing book! Concise, clear, very good points and appropriate anecdotes. Sound wisdom".

Eva Long
UC Davis MIND institute, USA

"Daniel has written a GREAT book! This book will be a very useful tool for young people. My job involves talking with college students one-on-one, and many times when talking to these students I discover that they are depressed, they don't know why they are here on Earth; don't know if they are valuable or if their existence matters at all. In my opinion, many times the root of their problem is not in their past (as psychoanalysts would say) but that they don't have hope and motivation for the future.

I believe this book would help a lot, because it gives very practical suggestions for what our attitude should be and what we actually should do. And most importantly, all this is on the basis of a relationship with God.
Thanks Dan for writing this book!"

Kis Mara
Campus Crusade for Christ
Budapest

'HOW TO CREATE THE FUTURE YOU WANT' is an inspiring book. A book needed for this generation.

Ade Omotunde
Language Difference Technologies
Milton Keynes

"I read this book and it's amazing, it's really substantial and inspirational. It's also very engaging and easy to read and comprehend"

Rutendo Chitiga, Author

"The book 'How To Create The Future You Want' is a book that must be read if you truly desire a great future. In this world of anxiety and fear many have lost hope for their future. This book will restore hope and courage to seek and create a great future. I greatly recommend this book for everyone and even for Parents and they will never be found wanting in the up bringing of their children".

Rev. Peter Oluwajoye
Senior Pastor, New Covenant Church
Camden Conference Centre

ACKNOWLEDGMENTS

This book has been in the making for over 3 years. Several times I stopped working on it but always found myself going back to writing and developing it, until it got to its final stage and ready to be published. It has been a very interesting experience and journey, one in which I have to acknowledge the help and contribution of several people.

Many thanks to God first of all for giving me the inspiration, resources, and tenacity to write this book and other books He is helping me to write. I must also specially thank my parents for the sacrifice they have made for me in the past, especially my sweet mum 'Mama' for her undying love and prayers.

Special thanks to my dear wife for her support and patience especially when I had to spend time on the key boards rather than with her. I would like to thank my wife's parents also, Mr and Mrs Jozsef and Katie Nafradi, as well as their other daughters, Katie and Marti for their encouragement and for letting me use their computer endlessly each time we visited them.

Many thanks also to Dr Lanre and Moji Tejuoso of Cloud 7 Ltd. The first script of this book was typed at Cloud 7. Special thanks also to 'Chief' Kolade Adebayo Oke who read through my book in its rough stages and gave me great support (God bless you dearest Chief for all your love and encouragement). Many thanks also to all my very dear friends (Tony Aisien, Deacon Julian, Brother Peter, Tayo Lawal, Zuberu, Cyril, Emma, Grace, Prince, Susan, Safi, Natasha, Obi,) and many more I couldn't write their names because of space.

My very special thanks goes also to my dear pastors, Rev. Peter and Pastor Kemi Oluwajoye, Pastor Ayo and Pastor Dupe Gbaja, and the entire members of The New Covenant Church, Camden Conference Centre for their love, support, and believing in me and giving me an opportunity to serve. Your are all a big part of my life.

Lastly, to Daniel Cooke and the other staffs at AuthorHouse for their excellent support in making sure this book was a finished product.

God bless you all.

Contents

"A life spent making mistakes is not only more honourable, but more useful than a life spent doing nothing"- George Bernard Shaw

"The journey of a thousand miles begins with one step"-Chinese proverb

"A mind is a terrible thing to waste"

"All things are possible to him who believes"-The Bible (Mark 9:2)

FORWARD

The greatest concern of man is the future. The words 'worry' and 'anxiety' exist because the future exists. The difficulty of predicting the future accurately by any mathematical means has put the burden of creating it on each individual.

Most of what we pursue in life is aimed at creating almost a perfect future, a tomorrow of our dream. God in His holy word, the Bible tells us He has a plan for us, a plan of peace and not of evil to give us a hope and a future – Jeremiah 29:11. However, God is not a magician; He created us as 'creatures of our own will.' Therefore we have a role to play in arriving at this great and beautiful future.

There is therefore a divinely structured future for us. It may seem our future is currently fractured or ruptured but by cooperating with your creator, you can nurture yourself into the divinely structured future.

This is what Daniel has outlined in this easy to read and easy to understand book. I strongly recommend the book for both your reading and study.

Timothy Kolade
National Overseer
New Covenant Church, UK

INTRODUCTION

Overtime I have developed the habit of observing people, situations, and events. I am always amazed to see how much each individual has been given the opportunity, resources, ability, and responsibility to live life as they wish and create the future they want. While a lot of factors may determine the various events, circumstance and outcome of our lives, the biggest influence in it all is you. You are the number one factor and influence in your life. This is the reason why no one can blame society or someone else for the way their life turns out or is shaped. There might be a few exceptions especially in the case of children or people who never had the chance to make a choice on what direction or shape their life takes. But this accounts for a few exception and in most other situation, every man or woman, young or old, is faced with the responsibility of making choices and decisions; forming habits and attitudes; developing relations and aptitudes, that would eventually and ultimately form or create the type of lives and future they end up having.

I have written this book …

- For the young man and woman who desires and seek to have a great future
- For the young man and woman who though they are not sure what kind of future they yet want but know something great awaits them if only they would believe and reach for it

- For the middle age man and woman who have not yet realised their dreams and the future they desire- there still remains great hope and possibilities
- For the elderly man or woman who are not content with the life they now have-its not over until its over
- And for anyone who may not be aware or sure of what the future hold for them...*you can create the future you want*

Whatever your stage or level in life, this book would help you:

- Believe in your God given dreams
- Recognize and fully utilize your potentials to achieve them
- Show you how to create the future you want
- Take responsibility for the direction of your life and not leave the issue of your personal success to chance or fate.
- Identify practical steps to take towards the attainment of your dreams.
- Find the motivation and inspiration to go the distance and do the things necessary to achieve the future they plan and hope to have.

It is my desire that this book will help you find the courage to believe in your dreams and the passion to create the future you really want.

1
Why You Didnt Remain A Baby

"When I was a child, I spoke like a child; I thought like a child, I reasoned like a child. When I became a man, I gave up childish ways." I Corinthians 13:11(English Standard Version)

Babies are such a pleasant and wonderful sight to behold. To watch them smile, hear them giggle; see them trying out new things like crawling or walking always bring laughter and joy. I have never seen anyone who didn't want to look at or hug a baby. However, as beautiful and adorable as they may be, babies don't remain babies. They grow! They develop into toddlers; adolescents; teenagers; and then adults.

It is tragic when babies don't grow. It is considered retarded growth. This happens when for some biological reasons a baby's ability to grow and develop is rendered impotent. When this happens the affected baby remains a baby in size even when they are old enough to be adults. An adult trapped in a baby's body could be a terrible defect to experience. But even more tragic than this is a baby trapped in an adult's body!

The need to grow is an essential requirement in life. Physical growth is a basic expression of life. But more important than physical growth is the emotional and mental growth of a person. A person is considered immature if they have not developed in this area. Have you ever been around an adult who still acted like they were a kid? I bet you got irritated or uncomfortable. Such feeling is only natural. We expect people to at least act their age and earn their due respect. This is because no one is expected to remain a child or still exhibit the traits of one when they are suppose to be grown ups. It may have been wonderful to be a child once, but it would be tragic to remain one because of two reasons.

1. WHATEVER DOESN'T GROW DIES

Growth is evidence of life. When something doesn't grow it's probably because it is dead or dying. When you were born your parents expected you to grow. At school your teacher expected you to grow. When you started working your boss expected the same. Growth doesn't stop when we are fully developed physically. Mental and emotional growth continues for the rest of our lives.

2. GROWTH IS THE PROMISE OF A FUTURE

When something grows it doesn't only express life or ability, it also holds the promise of a future. When parents see their child growing what comes to their mind is the future of that child. When owners of a business see the business growing what comes to their mind is expansion and profit. When a farmer sees his seed growing what comes to his mind is the harvest. Whatever grows holds the promise of a future. This is why the death of a young person is very painful because someone has been denied a future.

Life may have been so beautiful as baby or a child. Having no need to worry about paying bills; getting a job; choosing a career or wondering what people thought about you were part of the benefits of being a child. But soon you grew up. Then you knew responsibility and pressure. You were faced with challenges and had to make your own decisions. You realized you had to live your life and no one could live it for you. You discovered people are not always as nice as they first seem. You experienced disappointments with people. Ah! You knew what it felt like to make mistakes and suffer the consequences of a bad decision.

You may even wonder why the world is the way it is. What happened to the world you knew as a sweet little baby? Welcome to the real world! This is the point when a person is initiated into an adult's world. Where childhood is left behind and new life skills are learnt. If a young man or woman has grown emotionally and mentally they may be prepared to face life as adults at this point, but if the opposite is the case life may become a nightmare. This is *where* some young people fail or succeed in life. We would deal with *why* in other chapters.

I remember the story of a young man in his early 20's who committed suicide in the fall of 2005 because he couldn't cope with the pressures and challenges he was facing any longer. If only someone showed him the way? If only someone taught and helped him to grow and develop the life skills he needed to succeed as a young man: knowing how to handle the pressures and challenges life may throw at him? He probably would have still been alive to go on and do something worthwhile with his life.

There are three very important reasons why you couldn't remain a baby and why you had to grow. An understanding of these reasons would certainly help you appreciate life better than you have ever had before:

1. LIFE IS A RESPONSIBILITY

Babies have no responsibilities. They have no worries. They have no plans or thought for tomorrow. They are cared for by someone else. All their needs are met by someone else. Give them a bottle of milk and toys to play with and they are '*happy forever*'. But when they get older or become adults they know responsibility. They become exposed to choices and challenges. And sometimes it seems life isn't fair or wonderful anymore. It takes an adult that has been prepared and equipped both mentally and physically to succeed in a world like ours today. Only a prepared man or woman can face the diverse challenges and responsibilities life would throw at them. I have seen many young people lose hope and give up in life because they couldn't cope with the challenges and responsibilities. I have also seen middle age people who threw in the towel because they couldn't go on any longer. The problem wasn't what they faced. It was the fact that they were unprepared for life's challenges and responsibilities.

2. LIFE IS AN ADVENTURE

The ups and downs, difficulties and pressures we all face in life expresses one truth: Life is an adventure we must live. If we lack this understanding, we would only see the pains, disappointments and challenges we face as adversities and lose heart. But life is an adventure and until we learn how to live through it we are in for a hard time. And believe me, adventures are not for babies-and life is full of many unpredictable adventures. If you are tempted to dismiss this fact, just take a look at your own life. Recall those experiences where you thought there was no way out. But then there was a twist. And you thought you were lucky and wonder how you survived?

Helen Keller (1880-1968), famed blind and deaf activist, author and lecturer explains it this way: *"Life is either a daring adventure or it is nothing at all."*

3. LIFE IS AN OPPORTUNITY

Think about it? Hundreds of thousands of people die every day. Many babies never made it to their first birthday. A lot even lost their chance or life still yet in the womb. But you are alive and can still hope and plan for another day. Every one who is alive today has an advantage over those who are dead. Life is an *opportunity* you can't afford to waste or misuse. You may say you don't know what's going to happen to you tomorrow and as a result not want to expect too much in life or dream or make big plans. But that's as good as playing dead. Douglas Macarthur, American military leader and World War II veteran said, *"There is no security on this earth, only opportunity."* Your life is an opportunity to learn. To give, to love, to find meaning and fulfil purpose. H. Jackson

Browne, renowned singer and songwriter of the early 70's said, *"Don't be afraid to go out on a limb. That's where the fruit is".*

YOU ONLY LIVE ONCE...MAKE THE MOST OF IT

No one has the opportunity to live the same life twice. We only live once. We don't have a choice on that. But we have a choice and responsibility to decide how we live our lives and what kind of future we would have. As a child your parents may have planned your life or may be they never did. But as an adult, your future is entirely up to you. I once heard someone say, *"If you fail, it's your fault. If you succeed, it's your fault. So choose carefully the fault you want to bear"*

WHY YOU DIDNT REMAIN A BABY FOLLOWUP EXERCISE

In what areas of your life would you say you have experienced adequate growth?

What is your definition of maturity?

How would you best describe your attitude when you face challenges and obstacles in life?

How would you describe life as a responsibility everyone has to bear?

How would you describe life as an adventure you must live?

How would you describe life as an opportunity you have been given?

2
YOUR FUTURE HAS ALREADY BEGUN!

"Where there is no hope in the future, there is no power in the present."
- John Maxwell

Many people wait for the future to happen. They live and spend their lives in expectation of a day or an event or a time yet to come. To most people the future is an indefinite time still far away. But what most of us fail to realize is that the future has already begun. It is not waiting to commence. It has already started. For some other people, the future they once anticipated is already past. Whatever may be your ideas or definition of the future, its imperative you understand that you are ultimately responsible for the future you would experience or already experiencing. Though the term 'Future' sounds like a distant time or event, our futures have already begun.

For most people it may sound strange to hear that they can create the future they want. It may even be an unusual or unacceptable thing to do or attempt. I have talked with a lot of people who believe *'whatever will be will be, what's the need to really try'*. But that's the same reason only 5% of the worlds population are able to live the kind of life they dream of and enjoy the type of future other's envy. The other 95% still consider it unusual to create their own future and may never enjoy the kind of future they really desire in their hearts. Nevertheless the fact remains that deep down in our hearts we all desire a better life and future for ourselves. You can create the future you want! Yes it's possible to achieve your dreams and enjoy the success your heart desires.

Creating the future you want means *choosing; envisioning; planning; and actively pursuing* the type of life you desire to have. This implies two things; 1.You are not leaving your life to chance or fate to decide the outcome of it. 2, you are productively and actively engaged in making the things happen necessary to create the life you desire. Observe the life of any successful or fulfilled person, you would see these same factors as part of the major core principles responsible for the life they have and enjoy. Let's take a closer look to what it means to create the future you want.

CHOSING YOUR FUTURE

A successful life or future does not just happen. Neither do people wake up one day to find out that they have a great future or life. A successful future starts with the deliberate choice to have one. We all make choices in life and reap the benefits or consequences of the choices we've made. Whether it's with a career; a spouse; the place we live; the friends we keep; or the habits we develop, a choice was involved. In the same way, when it comes to the quality of future we will have, a choice is required.

Choice consists of the mental process of thinking involved with the process of judging the merits of multiple options and selecting one for action. In very simple words therefore, we are faced with several options in life (what to do, who to become, the type of future we want, where we want to go, the friends we keep, etc). Research proves that every person makes an average of 2,500 choices every single day. We have the sole responsibility of making informed choices and decisions in our day to day life. We are responsible for the choices we make and in turn our choices are liable for how our lives turn out. We must learn to choose the type of life we want and follow a definite course of action to experience it. This differentiates a wish from a choice. For example I choose to be an author and write books. I could have spent valuable time watching TV or doing other things out of line with my desire to be an author and never write a book. I would end up becoming a wishful author who never wrote any book.

Success is a choice. So also is failure. Whatever we do is govern by a choice. And to not make any choice at all is also a choice. Don't make the mistake of going through life without knowing what you want or where you want to be? Elaine Maxwell said, *"My will shall shape the future. Whether I fail or succeed shall be no man's doing but my own. I am the force; I can clear any obstacle before me or I can be lost in the maze. My choice; my responsibility; win or lose, only I hold the key to my destiny."*

Have you made a definite choice about the type of future want? You can only create the future you have chosen. Our lives are a reflection of both conscious and subconscious choices we have made. 5 or 10 years from now you would be where you are and who you are because of the choices you are making today. This is the first step to creating the future we want-by choosing it. The question is: have you made a clear-cut choice about what kind of future you want or you just have a vague idea? Do you want to own your own business? Do you want to go to college and get a degree? Do you want to pursue a career in a particular field or industry? Do you want to be financially independent? What do you really want to do with your life? Dr. Myles Munroe, renowned author and speaker said, *"People fail because they don't know what they want to succeed in."* You stand a better chance in life when you have made a definite choice about the type of life and future you want.

ENVISIONING YOUR FUTURE

The second step to creating the future you want is keeping a *Vision* of the future you desire and have chosen constantly in your mind. Vision is far more than just the ability to see. It involves the ability to create a desired or preferred picture of something that has not yet happened or come to pass. We must envision the type of future we want for us to be able to eventually have and experience it.

To envision your future means to have and hold a mental picture of the future you desire- not occasionally but constantly. It involves the use of our God given imaginative abilities to visualize the things we want to happen in our lives. The Bible states in Proverbs 29:18 *"where there is no vision the people perish"*. A major reason people get very frustrated in life and seem to have no passion or sense of direction is the lack of a vision. You possibly won't want to look forward to a life or future you can't see, or when all you see is something negative. Helen Keller, one of the most inspiring women that ever live said, *"The most pathetic person in the world is someone who has sight but has no vision"*. An amazing truth about Helen Keller was that she was blind as a baby when she was only 18months old. But she went on to write 11 books; promoted the course of women rights; and was a lecturer and reformer. There is no limit to what your life can become if you can learn to envision the future you want.

Can you imagine what your life or future would be like? Do you have a mental picture in your mind of what your life would be like 5-10 years from now? Some people can't even imagine what their lives would be like 12 months from now. It's easier to envision your future if you have already made a choice about the kind of future you want. One of the reasons God gave us a mind is so we can think creatively and use our imaginative abilities to achieve the things we desire. The truth is we can accomplish whatever our minds can imagine. William Arthur Ward, an American famous writer and scholar said, *"If you can imagine it, you can create it. If you can dream it, you can become it."*

Our lives have a way of taking the shape of the visions we hold in our hearts. That's why we must choose the kind of future we want and constantly envision that future in our mind. The major benefits of envisioning the future we want are 1. We find a sense of direction and focus in the things we do. 2, the vision or picture in our mind inspires and fills us with passion to reach for our dreams. 3, we develop a resourcefulness to deal with situations and challenges that may come our way.

PLANNING YOUR FUTURE

This is the next important step in creating the future you want. The dictionary defines a plan as *"A scheme, program, or method worked out beforehand for the accomplishment of an objective or goal".* Creating the future you want would involve quite a lot of planning. This is where a lot of people lose tenacity and focus. It takes discipline and some degree of good thinking to come up with a good plan. People don't generally plan to fail in their lives. They simply fail to plan. If you don't have a plan for your life and future, it becomes easier to get distracted and miss the mark. If you've planned nothing, then that's exactly what you'll get. Nothing!

In the context of creating the future you want, planning is the whole process of *setting goals, developing strategies, and outlining tasks and schedules* necessary to help you achieve the future you have chosen and envision in your mind. This process as you can tell involves details and documentation. Any plan for your future that lacks these ingredients is really not a plan.

Setting goals. This is a key part in planning and creating your future. A goal is a clear objective or purpose toward which an endeavour is directed. It is an end in mind. A goal must be clear, specific, written and have deadlines. What are your goals in life? What financial, career, or relationship targets have you set for yourself and when do you intend to accomplish them? We would talk more about goals and how to achieve them in a later chapter.

Developing strategies. You must have or develop strategies you can use to achieve your plans and dreams. A strategy is simply a course of action you intend to follow in order to achieve your plan or set goals. It involves reasoning and consulting. You don't need to be a genius or expert to have a good strategy. Talking with some one who is better skilled or experienced at what you intend to accomplish could be a good source of developing your own strategies.

Outlining task. This are the specific assignments you would need to undertake to achieve the plans you have made. They may include taking a specific class, undergoing a required training or performing a particular function on a periodic or regular basis. They could be easy or difficult. A good question to ask yourself is: "what are the important task necessary for me to undertake to be able to accomplish my plans?"

Scheduling. This aspect of planning bothers more on your ability to organize your time so that you can focus on your priorities and things that are more important to you. It involves setting feasible deadlines to your goals and task. Proper scheduling would help you achieve 3 things. 1, prevent you from having indefinite plans and goals. 2, help you stay organize in view of your priorities so you don't spend time on what's not important. 3, keep you on track as you attempt to accomplish the goals you have set for yourself.

PURSUING YOUR FUTURE

The phrase *pursue* explains itself. You could observe the other three aspect of creating your future (*choosing, envisioning, and planning*) but if you fail to actively pursue the future you want you may as well just be daydreaming. You would need to chase what you want. It's like falling in love with someone really beautiful and yet never make any real and engaging efforts to win her. You may even be rejected the first and second time you attempt to win her over, but it doesn't mean you give on your dream.

A major reason why most people never really get the type of future they want is because they have not truly given it their best shot. They try once, may be twice, may be even several times and give up because nothing happened or they didn't get the expected results. How sad it would be for them to discover they were just a few more attempts away from realizing their dreams. Thomas Edison, one of the greatest inventors that ever lived made 999 attempts to invent the electric light bulb and yet failed. What would have happened if he gave up trying one more time? He later on went to say, *"Many of life's failures are people who did not realize how close they were to success when they gave up."*

People fail in life for a number of reasons. A key reason is the lack of resilience. People give up too soon. A lot of people don't know what it means to persist long enough to get the results they want. The problem the lack of this quality has caused in the lives of many people is obvious. Most marriages fail because one or both parties are unwilling to put up with the issues or problems long enough to find the best way to resolve whatever the problems might be. Many new businesses didn't fail because they were meant to. The owners didn't just persist long enough for a change to happen. If you take a honest retrospect of your own life you would discover goals and desires you failed to achieve because you didn't have the necessary resilience to go through whatever you had to go through to get what you wanted. This quality marks the difference between those who get what they want and those who spend the rest of their lives dreaming of things they want and never have.

Resilience means the ability to recover quickly from shock, injury, and misfortune. It is also the ability to deal with change and retain an original state or form regardless of what happens. If you are going to create the future you want this is a quality you must develop. Dale Carnegie, one of Americans foremost personal development expert, speaker and author said, *Most of the important things in the world have been accomplished by people who have kept on trying, when there seemed to be no hope at all.*

You cannot predict or determine everything that would happen in your life or the days ahead of you. Changes are bound to happen. But if you have developed resilience you have the advantage to adapt to changes and make every situation work in your favour. This way, you would have both the tenacity and fortitude to create the future you want. It was Frank Llord Wright a pioneer and innovator in American Architecture that said, *"I know the price of success: dedication, hard work, and an unremitting devotion to the things you want to see happen"*.

YOUR FUTURE HAS ALREADY BEGUN! FOLLOWUP EXCERCISE

How would you define the term 'Future'?

What kind of future do you see yourself having?

In the next 5 years, where do you see yourself?

i.   Financially (financial independence, just comfortable, have your debts paid off to at least 50-80 percent, start a special saving for retirement)

ii. Professionally (top of your career, known for excellence in your chosen field or acquire a new skill, training)

iii. Spiritually (a matured person in your faith and belief, a mentor)

iv. Relationships (a strong and dependable person)

The above is only a guide. You may write down your own thoughts in the lines provided below.

What are the 3 most important things you would like to achieve in the next 12-24 months and how would achieving this things help you create the future you want?

  1.

  2.

  3.

3
JUST BEFORE YOU LEAVE THE HOUSE

Understanding the power of preparation

Peter just turned eighteen. He thought he was ready for what he was about to do-strike out on his own. He was smart and strong willed. "I can take care of myself and handle any challenge," he often told his mum. He left home full of determination to come back home soon enough with his own success story. He had everything worked out in his head.

20 years later, he finally realized things didn't turn out as he had hoped. "At least I tried, even though I missed it many times". But with every new day he wished he was more informed and better prepared before leaving the house. He wished he was patient to learn the lessons he needed to help him along the way.

Bola was only seventeen when she left home. She wanted the freedom and the opportunities that came with being independent. A few years later she returns home to her parents with tears in her eyes, a broken heart, an addition problem, and two beautiful kids. She pleaded to stay in the house until she could get back on her feet again.

FREEDOM COMES WITH A PRICE

I am not against freedom or independence. I actually think it is one of the best things that could happen to a young person. However freedom comes with a price. It must be prepared for. If the choice of independence is pursued without preparation and a willingness to accept responsibility, it could mean disaster and pose as a threat to a persons dream for a great future. For example, the freedom of speech gives everyone the right to say what they want or feel, but the abuse of such freedom often leads to devastating hurts to people and relationships.

The Bible in the book of Luke, in chapter 15 holds an interesting account of a young man who went to his father and said: *"Father, give me the portion of goods that falls to me".* What he wanted was right and good-*Independence.* But the problem was that he wasn't prepared for what he was asking. He got what he wanted. But after a few weeks or may be months at the most, *"he wasted his possessions with prodigal living…and he began to be in want."* The truth is we are no different from the Prodigal son. We want freedom. We pursue independence. But with a heart not prepared for it the result is always the same. We end up worse than we started…*wasting possessions and be in want.*

When I was 13 years old I went to a trade fair with my friends. I had saved up my allowance so I could spend some money. It was my first time of going to such a place without my parents or uncles. I was without any kind of supervision. With my own money in my pocket and no one to tell me what to do, I felt like the king in my little world. I ended up getting drunk (at just thirteen)! I still can't explain till date how I got home or if someone ever took me home. For a very long time after that incident, I didn't have any more allowances neither did I dare ask my parents if I could visit a trade fair.

THE RESPONSIBILITY OF INDEPENDENCE

Independence gives you the right and power of freedom. But when we exercise such independence without reason or accountability we destroy or lose the things we love the most, including our very own future. Independence is never an excuse for irresponsibility. The London Metro newspaper in 2005 wrote about a tragic incident about a drunken dad who allowed his 9-year-old son to drive the car on the motorway. The end was predictable. They had an accident. The dad died on the spot. The young boy sustained serious injuries.

Freedom is never an excuse for careless or reckless living. Neither is independence a reason for unaccountable and irresponsible behaviour. Every society is filled with people who misunderstand freedom and abuse their independence. In Britain, and in most other developed countries, it has been debated whether the age for the consent to have sex should be reduced from 16 years to 14 years. It is also being debated whether the right age for a teenager to buy alcohol should be reduced from 18 to 16 years. It should be never be a surprise why teenage pregnancies, STD, drunkenness, and socially unacceptable behaviour are on an alarming increase. Prison cells are being filled with more young adults than middle-aged adults today. The biggest threat of this trend is that a lot of people are ruining their own future before they ever get a chance to live it. What every young person desperately need is someone to teach and prepare their hearts for the freedom and independence they desire, and show them how to handle the responsibilities that comes with it. When this happens, the future of the young people in our society and families are better secured.

FREEDOM *VS.* A GREAT FUTURE

In an attempt to live a life of freedom countless number of people have ended up with a life of mediocrity and practically live the rest of their lives with no certain future in view. In an effort to enjoy freedom and live the way we want people with great potentials and talents have lost out from a promising future.

Mike Tyson is one of the greatest boxers ever to have graced the boxing world. A great talent and an unmatched boxing skill and strength were not enough to secure the great future his kind of skill and success attracted. Here's a brief biography about him.

"Mike Tyson is one of the most notorious boxers in prize fighting history thanks to his actions both inside the ring and out. His speed, power and angry aggression earned him the World Boxing Council heavyweight title in 1986, making him the youngest champion ever. The next year he won the World Boxing Association title and "Iron Mike" became the undisputed heavyweight champion of the world. In 1988, in one of his most famous fights, Tyson knocked out previously undefeated Michael Spinks in 91 seconds and earned $20 million. For a brief time he seemed invincible, until he was knocked out by the lightly regarded James "Buster" Douglas in 1990. Then Tyson began making headlines for different reasons: his brief marriage to actress Robin Givens was followed by a bitter divorce battle; he was convicted of rape in 1992 and spent three years in prison; a comeback was stymied in 1997 when he bit off a chunk of Evander Holyfield's ear in the middle of a match; he was jailed briefly again in 1999 for assault; and at a 2002 press conference to announce an upcoming bout, he attacked opponent Lennox Lewis and bit his leg. (The fight took place anyway on 8 June 2002, and Lennox knocked out Tyson in the eighth round). Tyson's fans considered him a troubled youth who battled long odds to become one the sport's greatest names; his detractors said his behaviour gave the sport a black eye. Tyson's fight career never quite recovered after his stint in jail, and he said he "most likely" wouldn't fight again after being defeated in a 7th-round technical knockout by journeyman heavyweight Kevin McBride on 11 June 2005

On the front page of the June, 2005 USA Today, Tyson is quoted as saying: "My whole life has been a waste - I've been a failure" Tyson has grossed an estimated $400 million in his career, but filed bankruptcy a couple of years ago."

Culled from answers.com

THE POWER OF PREPARATION

I personally believe the major reason Mike Tyson failed and lost both his career and fortune was the fact that he was never really prepared for the future. There's a big difference between preparing for success and preparing for the future and learning how to handle success when it comes. Preparing for success helps you develop the necessary talents and skills to succeed. But preparing for the future gives you the opportunities to both learn how to succeed and develop the behavioural patterns necessary to handle success when it comes. Denis Waitley, a leading keynote international speaker and business consultant said, *"Talent is inborn but behaviour is learnt"*. Talent alone cannot sustain success. It may attract a great future, but it can't preserve it. Tyson no doubt was well trained to fight, to win and succeed from his teenage years. But no one taught him how to live and handle success. No one showed him how to prepare for the future. He was accounted to own 90 exotic cars. Made 20 million dollars in 90 seconds from one fight. Earned 400 million dollars in his short career. Yet he lost everything before he was 38 years old.

The right type of preparation is essential if we are to create the future we want and more importantly preserve that future. We must not only prepare to succeed. We must also prepare to sustain success. To create the future you want both types of preparation are very important.

LEARN TO LIVE THE LIFE YOU WANT

The life you don't learn to live is hard to live. In other words it is more important for you to develop a quality before you need it and not wait until you need it before trying to develop it. To be a skilled surgeon, you don't wait until the day you are called to the operating room or theatre to develop the skills to save a life. To be a successful businessperson you don't wait until you start a business before you develop essential business skills and quality to run a business. You would have to develop these qualities and skills long before you set out to do the main thing. But what happens today is that people wake up one day and just decide to start a new business, job or career without first learning and developing the skills required to succeed in what they want to do. It's a little wonder why so many businesses fail and why so many people don't succeed at what they want to do.

The same principle applies when it comes to creating the future you want. You don't wake up one morning to the life you have been dreaming about. We must learn daily, grow daily, and develop the needed skills and qualities to be able to have and experience the kind of life and future we desire.

DON'T FORGET TO DO YOUR HOMEWORK

As a kid I hated homework and avoided doing them as much as I could. I ended up doing badly in class. After a while I picked interest in homework and did all my assignments. (I didn't want to be laughed at in class). My performance in school greatly improved and I thought I became clever overnight, but actually, I still had the same brains and abilities. My performance only improved because I paid attention to preparation. Robert H. Schuller said, *"Spectacular achievement is always preceded by spectacular preparation."*

Today, I know far better that if I'm going to do well in any endeavour I have to pay the price of preparing myself. Aristotle, the legendary philosopher said, *"We are what we repeatedly do. Excellence, then, is not an act, but a habit."* Henry David Thoreau, a noted American author and philosopher explained this further when he said *"I know of no more encouraging fact than the unquestionable ability of man to elevate his life by conscious endeavour"*. You can change your life and create the future you desire if you pay the price of preparing for the life you want to live. You can live your dreams and experience a great future if you make the effort.

TO FIND YOU MUST FIRST DEFINE

Each one of us has the responsibility and ability to choose and create the kind of future we want for ourselves. If you don't assume this responsibility, someone else or something else will, and you most certainly won't like the choice they will come up with. You must decide and define exactly what kind of future you want for yourself. It's always easier to find what you are looking for if you have a clear definition of it.

To make it easier for you to decide what kind of future you want (if you've not already), here are a few questions you should ask yourself and provide honest answers to:

1. What exactly do I want out of life?
2. Where would I be 5 years from now?
3. What dreams, plans and goals would I have if I were sure of the possibility of achieving them?

We must clearly define our goals to be able to achieve them or we may end up wasting a lot of time chasing the wrong priorities. Robert Heinlein, one of the most influential authors in science fiction said: *"In the absence of clearly defined goals, we become strangely loyal to performing daily trivia until ultimately we become enslaved by it".*

God has blessed every one of us with the potentials and the opportunity to be successful and great during our lifetime and to experience a great future. But to a large extent we have a role to play for this to happen. How well we engage the time and resources we've been given by God, and the extent to which we prepare our selves to get what we want out of life, play key roles in ensuring this happens. I recommend that every one seeking a great life and future to take time out to do four important things.

1. TAKE TIME TO DREAM

A man without a dream is a man without a future-one who has left his life to chance and fate. Jim Valvano, legendary American college basketball coach said, *"Be a dreamer. If you don't know how to dream, you are dead,"* America's most influential first lady, Eleanor Roosevelt, couldn't have put it better when she said: *"The future belongs to those who believe in the beauty of their dreams."* Go ahead. Take time out to dream. It's one of the best opportunities we have to paint tomorrow the way we like it, then pay the price and go for it. Don't dream small dreams-they never take any man far.

2. TAKE TIME TO LEARN

With every big dream comes the big responsibility to learn the 'ways' and the 'how' to make it happen. Can you imagine wanting to fly an airplane without learning how? Educate yourself for whatever you plan to become. Acquire the skills and the 'know how' to make things happen for yourself. You owe your future that responsibility. Read books. Listen to tapes. Attend seminars offering the information you need. Look for someone to mentor you. The average person doesn't like to learn something new if it involves much time and effort-that's why they are average.

3. TAKE TIME TO PLAN

Planning takes a lot of time but it's never wasted time or effort. 1 month of good planning can save you 1 year of wasted time, effort, resources and regrets. So many people live through life without making plans for the life they live. I've actually heard someone say, "I don't plan my day, week, or year. How do you expect me to have a lifetime plan?" Its no surprise some people don't make significant progress in life. "If you fail to plan, you've planned to fail"-proverb

4. TAKE TIME TO ACT

This is a very important aspect of deciding the future you want for yourself. You can have big dreams, learn all you can and make very good plans, but if you don't act, you will remain in the same spot for a very long time. Acting on a dream, plan, or idea is what makes the difference between ordinary dreamers and real achievers.

Thomas Edison, one of the greatest inventors the world has ever known-with his number of inventions reaching 1,093, once said; *"If we did all the things we were capable of doing, we would literally astound ourselves."*

JUST BEFORE YOU LEAVE THE HOUSE FOLLOWUP EXCERCISE

How prepared would you honestly say you are for the future you want?

What are your biggest dreams for the future?

What specific plans do you have in place to ensure the dreams and future you want come to pass?

List 5 tasks you may need to undertake to help you achieve your next major goal or dream and how would achieving this goal or dream help you create the future you want to create?

1.

2.

3.

4.

5.

4
EVERY ROAD HAS A MAP

"If you don't know where you are going, any road would take you there"

Have you ever tried to locate a place without having a clue on how to find it? Or travel to a place you've never been before without a description or map? There are few things as frustrating and energy draining as trying to reach a new destination without proper description. You'll end up going in circles and think you're getting somewhere or probably get missing. We stand the chance of facing a lot of frustration and discouragement when we compromise the importance of going along with a map or guide each time we try to reach a new destination.

THE FAST TRACK OF SUCCESS

There is nothing you want to do or accomplish that someone else has not done. Or at least they have tried something similar to what you are about to do or trying to succeed at. You would succeed faster and easier if you would take the time to learn from those who have already succeeded in something similar to what you want to do. Whenever you see someone who is already enjoying the kind of future you want, it would benefit you to stop and learn a few things from them. It will take humility and a teachable heart to do this. This attitude doesn't come easy with everyone but you would save yourself a great deal of time and wasted effort and resources if you learned from someone smarter than you. Isaac Newton, 16th century inventor and pioneer of physics who invented the Law of Gravity, in a letter to a friend in 1675 said, *"If I have seen further it is by standing on the shoulders of giants."* We all need *'giants'* on whose shoulders we can stand on. Whether your goal is financial independence or career success, there are *'giants'* already in that field. Instead of letting these giants (who are already successes in their own rights) scare or intimidate us, we can learn from their wealth of knowledge, experience, and trade secrets.

FIND A MENTOR

A mentor is a wise and trusted guide. A mentor is also someone that can give you valuable advice and counsel you with your best interest in his or her mind. They are not necessarily your friends or peers. You would benefit greatly by having someone to mentor you. The following are part of the advantages of having a mentor in your life:

A mentor will save you time and money

Mentors are often more experienced than their protégés or the people they teach. The years of experience, knowledge, and skill a mentor has acquired through the course of time can be easily taught or passed on to those they teach. Having the right mentor in your life will save you investing the same amount of time and resources they had to spend to gain the wisdom and experience they posses. It has taken someone like Sir Alan Sugar or Richard Branson over two decades of years to gain the business skill, experience and wisdom they have today. But if they had to mentor someone wanting to succeed in business it would probably take such a person or protégée far less time to succeed in their chosen field of business because they would teach you from mistakes they made in the past and ways they wasted time and resources chasing the wrong things and how you can save yourself time and money doing the right things from your first year in business.

A mentor will guide you through unfamiliar territories

Most people fail or give up when they chart through unfamiliar waters or territory. A mentor would have likely been through what you are going through and may have handled what you are having difficulties with. A task, challenge, or goal is easier to accomplish if you have a mentor to offer you valuable wisdom and counsel when you need it.

A mentor will tell you as it really is

This is where a mentor is different from a friend. A friend would cheer you on even when you are failing (what are friends for?) but a mentor will tell you as it is and show you why and where you are failing even if you are not happy to hear it. We need our friends to cheers us on when we are failing and we also need mentors to tell us why we are failing and show us how to succeed.

A mentor wouldn't make you succeed over night

While a mentor would be a great help to your life, having one doesn't mean you are going to achieve success over night or in a short matter of weeks. The ultimate responsibility to succeed still rest on us whether we have a mentor or not. A mentor simply makes the journey more resourceful and better.

A mentor does not guarantee that you wouldn't make mistakes

The fact that you have a mentor doesn't mean you are not going to make some mistakes along the way. You will-but may be less than you normally would. A mentor would teach, counsel and motivate you but key decisions and actions would be up to you. And remember, we are imperfect people living in a world that is not perfect. So expect to make some mistakes even if you have a mentor as they are no guarantee you would never make a mistake.

It is your responsibility to seek a mentor and develop a relationship with one

Mentors don't necessarily go around looking for protégés to teach and train. You would be fortunate to have one come looking for you. It is actually the other way round. It is your responsibility to look for someone who has what it takes to help you succeed in an area you have chosen to excel. The next time you come across someone who seem to know what you want to learn or have what you are trying to get, cultivate a mentor protégé relationship with them and learn as much as you can from them. Ask them what skills they had to develop; what obstacles they had to overcome; what price they had to pay to get to where they are. You would be surprised at how much you could end up learning from them without paying for it.

There are different types of mentors

There are financial mentors. Academic/professional mentors, relationship mentors, business mentors, and spiritual mentors. Every one isn't an expert on the same thing. You probably wouldn't need a financial mentor to tell you how to handle you marriage or relationships. You would need a business mentor to teach you how to start or effectively run a business. You have to find the right mentor for the right assignment.

You must have a willing and teachable heart

You can have the best mentor in the world and still not benefit or learn anything from him or her. We have a lot of people who seem to know it all and don't need anyone. But to benefit from a mentor, you must be willing to learn and have a teachable heart. We must drop our hats of knowledge and listen to the words of wisdom whenever we are in the presence of a mentor.

A LESSON FROM JESUS

In the New Testament of the Bible Jesus had 12 disciples He mentored for three and a half years. He constantly taught them both in private and in public. In public He seemed to prefer to use stories and parables to teach both his disciples and the public until one day His disciples decided to ask him why?

"The disciples came up and asked, 'Why do you tell stories?'"

He replied, 'you've been given insight into God's kingdom. You know how it works. Not everybody has this gift, this insight; it hasn't been given to them. Whenever someone has a ready heart for this, the insights and understandings flow freely. But if there's no readiness, any trace of receptivity soon disappears. That's why I tell stories: to create readiness, to nudge the people toward receptive insight. In their present state they can stare till doomsday and not see it, listen till they're blue in the face and not get it. I don't want Isaiah's forecast repeated all over again: Your ears are open but you don't hear a thing. Your eyes are awake but you don't see a thing..." (The Message Bible, Matt 13:11-14)

STOP GOING IN CIRCLES

Life is a journey. If you spend your time going in circles, you will never get anywhere. Progress requires movement in a definite direction. One that will give you the results you desire, plan, and work for.

The Bible holds an account of how the Israelites, after leaving Egypt for the promise land, went in circles for many months. They didn't make any progress (though they were making a lot of movements) during this time of going in circles. God had to disrupt this pattern of movement to enable them make progress in their journey: *"You have compassed this mountain long enough: turn you northwards."*-Deuteronomy 2:3.

HOW DO YOU KNOW IF YOU ARE GOING IN CIRCLES?

It's not too difficult to tell if you are going in circles in your life-if you will be honest. You are going in circles if:

> ➤ You keep getting results you don't like doing the same thing over and over again.
> ➤ You find no joy, excitement, or challenge in what you do.
> ➤ You are not sure where the path you are in, or what you are doing will take you.
> ➤ You can't find meaning or purpose in what you do but you have to keep doing it anyway but meanwhile you honestly don't see a future in what you are doing.
> ➤ You have been spending your life holding on to past glory, success, or achievement.
> ➤ You can't account for any significant change in your life (work, relationships, personal growth) in the last 5 years.

YOU STILL HAVE TIME ENOUGH TO BEGIN AGAIN

You can regain control of the direction of your life. You can stop going in circles. You can create the future you want. You have the ability to decide where you should go and take necessary steps to get there. Whether you are 18, 29 or 69 years, it's never too early or too late to change your direction. You can decide a future for yourself and go for it. Joe E. Lewis, actor and entertainer, famous for his many quotes, wisely said, *"You only live once, but if you work it right, once is enough."*

Here's how to live once and not have regrets when you look back on your life.

1. DECIDE YOUR DESTINATION

David Campbell, one of Australia's most accomplished poets said, *"If you don't know where you are going you will probably wind up somewhere else"*. Exactly where do you want to go in life? What do you want out of life? What precisely would you want your future to be or look like? If you are not sure what your dream is what are the chances you are going to live it some day? How can you find a thing if you are not sure of just what it is you are looking for? We always end up wasting a lot of time, effort and resources when we try to reach a destination we are not sure about. Don Gabor, New York Times best selling author and speaker said, *"When you know your destination, your chances of getting there are better than if you start the journey with only a vague idea of where you want to end up."*

2. FIND THE RIGHT MAP

You won't need many maps for one journey-only the right one. Knowing where you want to go is half the problem of your journey solved. The other half is knowing how to get there. If you have decided on a dream or a future for yourself, invest the required time and effort to get the necessary information before you set out. You can get useful 'map' materials from talking with people who have achieved great dreams in their lives especially when it's similar to the dream you have. Reading books and biographies of people who got to destinations they always wanted and achieved the future they dreamt of will hold valuable inspiration and information for you. Such information will always help you chart your own course to your destination and future.

3. PACK ONLY THE RIGHT MATERIALS

Excess and unnecessary luggage is responsible for many delayed journeys and arrivals. Lots of people pack their bags with things they don't require for their journey. In the context of this book, excess or unnecessary luggage refers to attempting to reach your destination with things that could delay, distract, or disrupt your journey such as wrong habits, negative attitudes, relationships, an attachment to the past, unwillingness to change, etc. It is important you travel as light as you can with only the things you need and will assist your getting to your intended destination.

4. DON'T RUSH YOUR JOURNEY

Every trip you make in life (especially the one in pursuit of a dream or a future) should be enjoyed-and why not. Hasty trips never make for pleasant journeys. Don't set too short a dead line for a big dream or a significant landmark in your future. You will build tension and frustration and disappointment when you don't meet such deadlines. Life is a long distance race, not a sprint you make a dash for. There are things you are meant to learn on the way; people you should meet; places to go, and many stops to make. Take your time and enjoy the trip.

EVERY ROAD HAS A MAP
FOLLOWUP EXCERCISE

In what ways would your current job, career, qualification, skill, experience, knowledge and contacts help you create the future you want?

Is there someone whose life and success inspires you to want to create the future you want? Why and how do they inspire you?

Outline 5 different ways you think you can greatly benefit from a relationship with a mentor who can help you succeed and create the future you want?

1.

2.

3.

4.

5.

What specific training, skill, knowledge and experience would you need to help you accomplish your dream or create the future you want?

5
MIND THE PIT FALLS

Avoid the traps… they won't avoid you

As you travel the road to the future and destination you desire, you will come across many pitfalls on the way. They will attempt to trap, truncate, delay, and even stop you from reaching your destination and creating the future you want if it is possible.

In this chapter 8 pitfalls are briefly discussed. There are more pitfalls than this that you might face that could stop you from achieving your dreams or creating the future you want. However the following pitfalls are major ones and if you can avoid them you can overcome any other one that may come your way.

1. FEAR

Some people never get to live their dreams or reach for a new future because they are so afraid. Fear has stopped more people from experiencing changes in their lives than any other factor. Some others are so afraid of tomorrow that they hold onto yesterday with both hands and none left to reach for a new future. The Bible says *"fear has torment"*-1 John 4:18. It is capable of keeping a person in the same spot all their lives. I once read of a woman who didn't leave her house for several years because she was so afraid of dogs (a dog once bit her when she went out).

Fear can immobilize you from having a future. Former US president Harry Truman puts it this way: *"The worst danger we face is the danger of being paralyze by doubts and fears."* We must overcome the fears that stand between us and the future we greatly desire. To succeed *"we must do the things we think we cannot do"* said Eleanor Roosevelt. Oprah Winfrey, TV giant and the world's richest woman said, *"I have a lot of things to prove to myself. One is that I can live fearlessly."*

2. PROCRASTINATION

This has kept a lot of people from their dreams of having and creating the future they want. Procrastination is the habit of putting off things until later that you could have done now, until you get them done too late or never at all. This habit accounts for the inability of many to make significant progress with their lives despite their great potentials. *"Procrastination is opportunity's natural assassin"* Victor Kiam revealed. How many things have you ended up not doing and lost precious opportunities as a result because you kept putting them off? Someone once said, *"The wise does at once what the fool does at last."*

John C. Maxwell, Leadership expert, author and speaker said, *"Procrastination steals a person's time, productivity and potential."* Don't let procrastination rob you of the future you dream of and plan for anymore. Start acting now.

3. INDICISION

The ability to be decisive is a trait common with most achievers and very successful people. Most people can't make up their minds on what they want, where they want to go, or what they want to do with their lives. You can't walk in two different directions at the same time. Guess what happens when you chase two rabbits? You lose both-not surprisingly. Be definite about what you want-it makes getting it a lot easier and quicker. You won't get the time and chance to get all you may want in life. Make up your mind on the ones that are more important to you and stay focused on getting it.

"A double minded man is unstable in all his ways."-The Bible (James 1:8)

4. CHARACTER DEFFECTS

As unpopular as it may sound today, the lack of character is a major reason why most people don't get what they want in life, and if they do, lose it after they get it. *"Character is what a man is in the dark."* said D. L Moody. It is the sum total of a person's values, attitudes, and habits revealed in his disposition. Your character determines who you really are, and who you are determines who and what you become.

Great charisma and talent never compensate for character defects. Mike Tyson was arguably the greatest heavy weight boxer the world ever knew. But he lost it all after two jail convictions resulting from different rape charges. Despite R. Kelly's extraordinary and continuous success as R & B biggest singer, songwriter and producer, his reputation is seriously held in question over court cases of child pornography and sex with a minor.

A friend of mine once told me his grandfather would always say: *"If you lose wealth, you've lost nothing; if you lose health; you've lost something; if you lose character, you've lost everything."*

5. WEAK COMITTMENTS

You will never accomplish anything of significant value without giving it your total commitment. Imagine if David Beckham or Tiger Woods were just involve in their games/careers and not committed to it 100%? Commitments separate doers from dreamers. If you are going to live the life you dream about and create the future you want the ability to make and keep commitments must be one of your benchmarks. If you say you are going to do something, at all cost and by all means, do it. If you set a goal for yourself, don't give up until you accomplish it. If you make a promise, keep it. Let your words be your bounds.

You may have big dreams, great goals and a desire for a wonderful future but until you are committed to making it happen, nothing happens. We must do what is required to get what we desire. *"When you are interested in something"* says Kenneth Blanchard, renowned author and speaker, *"you do it only when it's convenient. When you are committed to something, you accept no excuses, only results."*

6. THE WRONG CROWD

There are a few things as wrong as being in the wrong crowd when you are trying to reach the right destination. You will never get to the right place following the wrong crowd. As a matter of fact, we never get much done if we are always with the crowd, much less a wrong one. Someone once said, *"If you must conduct the orchestra, you should turn your back to the crowd."*

Have you noticed that you soon become like the people you hang out with the most?

We naturally tend to think, talk, and act like the company we keep. It's called the law of association. You will move further away from the dreams and the type of future you plan to have by keeping company with people that are not like minded. It's better to choose and keep the company of people who will inspire the dreams you have and bring you closer to the future you desire. Solomon, one of the wisest men who ever lived and author of the book of Proverbs said, *"He that walks with the wise shall be wise, but a companion of fools shall be destroyed."-The Bible (Proverbs).*

7. THE WRONG TIMING

Timing is important in everything we do in life. *"To everything there is a season, and a time to every purpose under the heaven."* The Bible (Ecclesiastes 3:1). To do the right thing at the wrong time or the wrong thing at the right time, will both lead to getting the wrong results. Some people work when they should actually rest, and rest when they ought to be working, and wonder why they don't do so much or get the results they want. Going to the university when you already have a family may be a good dream to help you get a great future. But the time you've chosen to do this could generate difficulties in other important areas of your life such as family, work, and finances. Choosing the right time to do the right things will produce the kind of results we want.

8. THE WRONG ADDICTION

Addictions are powerful. The right ones could make a man. The wrong ones can destroy him too. You could even reach the place of your dreams and be on top, only to lose it in one moment because of one addiction.

One of the greatest football legends of all time, Diego Maradona, lost his football fame and career because of an addiction problem. In October 2005, one of the world's most exceptional models, and Britain's best model faced the biggest challenge of career, and possibly the worst embarrassment ever because of a drug related picture of her on the front cover of the Sun newspaper. In less than 5 weeks after the release of that picture, she lost modelling and advert contracts totalling 18 million pounds sterling. Countless number of other great or "would-be great" persons have lost it because of the same problem. Millions more may never even come close to realizing their dreams because of the wrong addiction.

One of the saddest addiction stories is Whitney Houston. The following is part of an article culled from the UK's Sun Newspaper:

"SUPERSTAR Whitney Houston has spiralled into a world of squalor and degradation on deadly crack" as the shocking pictures in today's Sun newspaper reveal.

It shows the disgusting mess in the singer's bathroom after a drug binge.

Drug paraphernalia including a crack-smoking pipe, rolling papers, cocaine-caked spoons and cigarette ends are strewn across the surface tops.

But Whitney, 42, no longer cares.

She was one of the biggest female artists of her generation — with a string of '80s and '90s hit singles like I Wanna Dance With Somebody and more than 100million albums sold.

Now she is a paranoid wreck hopelessly hooked on crack.

Drugs have devastated her once-famous beauty. She is haggard, with dark circles under her eyes and a deranged look on her face.

She regularly disappears for days and weeks at a time — holed up in seedy crack dens in dangerous parts of town.

And she has blown much of her multi-million pound showbiz fortune on her habit.

Now family and friends fear the addiction will end in her death unless she can beat it."

(Source: The Sun.co.uk, 2006)

I strongly believe there's great hope for a talented person such as Whitney as long as the effort is made to overcome the habit or addiction. There's certainly a chance for any one who has an addiction problem if the commitment is made to overcome the problem.

There are all kinds of addiction to different things ranging from addiction to drugs, sex, smoking, gambling, alcoholism, pornography, excessive spending, too much TV, food and sleep. These addictions could stop a person from achieving their dreams and the future they desire or losing it when they get it.

YOU'VE GOT WHAT IT TAKES TO OVERCOME

Whatever pitfall, personal challenge or obstacle we may face along the way to creating and experiencing the type of future we greatly desire for ourselves, I strongly believe we have what it takes to overcome them. In my personal life I daily have to battle with overcoming procrastination. Looking back in my life, I could have written more books, started more businesses, achieved much more if I only didn't allow the convenience of procrastination. I didn't even realise it was a problem until a few years back. Sometimes I still procrastinate using *'waiting for the perfect timing'* as a disguise or excuse, but like I said, I battle daily to completely overcome this pitfall in my personal life. I am better than last year and certainly better than a few years back. Until I overcome this pitfall I won't relent.

There's much more that you can be and much more that you can do than you are doing at the moment. You have not even scratched the surface of your potential yet. Scientist say man has only succeeded in using just 5% of the brain. That means the average person is using less than 5% of their true mental capacity. You have what it takes to be all you were born and destined to be.

MIND THE PITFALL FOLLOWUP EXCERISE

What would you consider to be the pitfalls in your life stopping you from achieving the things you desire and creating the future you want?

In what ways do you think you can overcome these pitfalls?

Outline 4 strengths you may need to develop to consistently help you overcome the pitfalls you would come across as you attempt to achieve your dreams and create the future you want?

1.

2.

3.

4.

6

A GREAT IDEA COULD CHANGE YOUR LIFE

You will need many good ideas along the way

GREAT IDEAS COME AT ODD TIME

Have you ever tried hard at getting a good idea when you needed it the most and nothing was coming? Then you relax, and may be even forget about it. And then after some time-WOW! That great idea comes-when you weren't expecting it.

I can't explain it and I'm yet to come across anyone who can-great ideas come at odd times! From the middle of your sleep; when you're in the bathroom; having breakfast or lunch; discussing an unrelated topic; jogging; swimming; and when you're even laughing to a joke or watching a game or video, a great idea always seem to pop up in your head-when you least expect it.

HOW DO YOU EXPLAIN?

The law of Gravity- Isaac Newton was sitting under an apple tree when one of its fruit dropped on his head. He started wondering why the apple did not float upwards but had to fall downwards. He started thinking and working on the problem, and voila! He discovered the law of gravity.

The blue jeans- Levi Strauss went to California during the "GOLD RUSH" of 1848 in search of gold. Only 21 years old and a cloth seller, he took a few cloths to sell on the journey to survive. He sold all the cloths he had except a roll of canvas-no one wanted cloths made of canvas. It turned out that the cloths of miners wore out quickly during digging. So Strauss had to make some canvas trousers to sell to them-the miners rushed for it! Not very satisfied with canvas, Levi Strauss started using a new fabric from Genoa, Italy, called "genes". He changed the name to "Jeans", and went later to call the pants he made "LEVI'S". From then he created his own "GOLD MINE" and didn't have to dig anymore.

KEEP YOUR EYES, EARS, AND MIND ALWAYS OPENED

You will need a lot of great ideas as you pursue your dreams and take the steps necessary to create the future you want. Keep your eyes, ears and mind opened. Your next great idea could pop up when you least expect it. It's advisable you always have a pen and a paper with you to make notes of these ideas. When you don't make note of them, you end up forgetting them.

YOU ARE ONLY A FEW IDEAS FROM YOUR BIGGEST BREAKTHROUGH

Are you working hard on your dreams and your goals but getting frustrated because things are not turning out as you hoped? Don't give up yet. You are only a few great ideas from the breakthrough you need.

It took Thomas Edison 1,000 tries to finally invent the light bulb. He never considered himself a failure the many times he failed before getting the right idea for his invention. Thomas Edison later went on to say: *"Genius"*, he said, *"is 99% perspiration and 1% inspiration"* towards the later end of his life and career, he also declared that *"Many of life's failures are people who did not know how close they were to success when they gave up."*

HOW THE MONOPOLY WAS INVENTED

In the early 1930's an unemployed engineer named Charles B. Darrow devised an intricate real estate board game to pass the time and take his mind off his financial problems. The game was played with dice, "deeds", "hotels", and "houses". He got several more ideas from failing real estate investment at that time. He kept developing his idea for the game and enjoyed playing it with his friends. He called the game monopoly.

Others soon heard of the game and ordered sets of their own. Darrow went on to produce hand made copies of monopoly at $4 a piece. When demand for the game grew beyond his ability to fill orders, he took the game to Parker Brothers who first rejected it because there were 52 design errors. Undaunted, he continued to produce handmade editions of his game and was highly successful

Parker Brothers caught wind of the success and decided to buy the rights to the game in 1935. At a point during that time Darrow's game was selling 20,000 sets a week. He became a millionaire. Today over 600 million people have played monopoly. It remains a classic as well as the world's most popular board game. All this was simply the result of one man's idea.

TURN YOUR IDEAS INTO A GOLD MINE

Your ideas could make you a lot of money plus provide you with a wonderful future. Your life is probably better today because of somebody's idea-and you are likely paying for it. The clothes you wear; the car you drive; the TV programs you enjoy; books you read; the mobile phone you use, and about everything you use that makes life more convenient for you is the product of somebody's idea. You pay for their idea and they get richer for it. How about if you start coming up with your own ideas and get paid for it?

There are three simple ways you can generate your own ideas and work on them until they are good enough to get you results:

1. THINK IT

Take out time to think up ideas. There's genius and creative ability within you. You are either not scratching deep enough or you are ignoring your genius ability. Charles Darrow never knew he was a genius until he came up with a game called "Monopoly". Be careful not to disregard your own ideas or throw them 'out the window' because somebody else thinks it's not a good one or considers it a joke. People often come up with original ideas intended as a joke. When Bill Gates, the founder of Microsoft first came up with the idea of having a desk top computer in every home using software from his company, people laughed at the idea. Never throw an idea away-it may be a lost opportunity.

2. INK IT

They say the *"Faintest line is stronger than the longest memory"*. You may never get the chance to remember a great idea a second time if you didn't take the time to document it the first time. I have had many brilliant ideas since I was a teenager. I can't remember most of them today, but I am sure if I made a note of most of the ideas I have had over the years I may have had some inventions to my name-you never know! Write down your ideas. Don't leave them in your head alone. They may not be there when you need it. Imagine if Charles Darrow only invented monopoly in his head and played it there, and never had to put down the ideas he had about the game? Write down your ideas. You may not need it now, but you'll have something properly documented to refer to when you need it. Besides, this will give you the opportunity to work and improve on your ideas in a very organized manner.

3. ACT IT

Don't waste time before acting on your ideas. Someone in Japan or India may have a similar idea too (no one has a monopoly of ideas). If you don't act fast, they may have the advantage and enjoy the benefits. Walt Disney, founder of the Walt Disney empire and Disney Land gave a very good advice on this note which he practiced himself to achieve the things he did: *"Get a good idea and stay with it. Dog it and work at it until its done and done right"* -Walt Disney -.

A GREAT IDEA COULD CHANGE YOUR LIFE FOLLOWUP EXCERISE

Make a list of your ideas you have. Don't worry if they seem unrealistic or impossible; just put them down in writing. Remember some of the best inventions were once unrealistic ideas that were laughed and crossed out.

In what ways do you think your ideas can improve your life or help make life better for someone else?

Are you willing and ready to invest the needed time and resources to make your ideas work and become a reality? If the answer is yes, how do you plan to invest the needed time and resources to make your ideas work?

7
Don't Let A Mistake Stop You

"A life spent making mistakes is not only more honourable, but more useful than a life spent doing nothing"- George Bernard Shaw

We all hate the idea of making mistakes. We want things to be done right the first time. "It has to be perfect or at least almost perfect" seem to be our watchword when we do things or supervise others doing things. We criticize those who make mistakes and we dread making them ourselves to avoid embarrassing ourselves before others. Well, have you ever imagined that a mistake could be a good thing to happen? Or consider the possibility of a mistake turning out to be a blessing? There are many positive and great lessons to learn from mistakes that were made in the past and those that may be made in the future. We should never be afraid of making mistakes but rather look out for the lessons we can learn from the mistakes we make. And we must learn not to criticize others for their mistakes also. There might just be a lesson or two for you to learn from their experience.

THE MISTAKE OF THE LIQUID SOAP
I'm sure almost everyone in the world today has used a liquid soap, either to have a bath, wash clothes, do their dishes or do something. But have you ever considered how the liquid soap came about? It was the result of a huge mistake!

After work one evening, a factory worker forgot to turn off the machine he worked with that produced powdered soap. The factory happened to be located by a beach. By the next morning when workers turned up for work, the machine had turned out so much soap that it extended to the shore of the beach. It was a disaster-or so they thought. When residents of the small town came to the scene they joked that no one will need to buy soap for the next couple of weeks as there was enough soap mixed with water by the beach shore. Children were already having fun bathing in the "soap water". While the workers were lamenting over the mistake and wondering what they will do if the factory was closed down because of the huge loss, the factory owner hit on a new idea "LIQUID SOAP" and thought he could create a permanent business from this huge mistake. He did just that and experienced a better business success than he imagined.

MISTAKES COULD BRING YOU A FORTUNE
Conventionally people say, 'Mistakes could cost you a fortune'. I like to see it the other way: "Mistakes could bring you a fortune". Mistakes could actually be blessings in disguise if you consider how some inventions, discoveries, businesses and breakthroughs came about.

DISGUISED BLESSINGS
Christopher Columbus
When he left the shores of the then Great Britain, he meant to sail to Asia, not America. But accidentally (or mistakenly we might say) he discovered America. And like they say, "the rest is history".

Coca cola
In 1886 John Pemberton, a pharmacist, cooked up a medicinal syrup in a large brass kettle. He and his assistant mixed the syrup with iced water and sipped it. He figured the syrup he had created was a fine tonic for people who were tired, nervous or plagued with sore teeth. The taste was good so they wanted some more. But this time his assistant accidentally used carbonated water to mix the second batch. Instead of medicine,

this time the result was a fizzy beverage, which became "Coca-Cola". Today an amazing 1 billion drinks are consumed from Coca cola each day. What a mistake!

Penicillin
Scientist Alexander Fleming in 1928 noticed that mold spores had contaminated one of the bacteria he had left by an open window. His experiment was ruined, or so he thought. But instead of discarding what was considered a mistake, he took a closer look and noticed the mold was dissolving the harmful bacteria. The result of his observation was a medical breakthrough-PENICILLIN!

DON'T WORRY ABOUT MISTAKES
You will do yourself great good not to worry much about your mistakes-both the ones you have made in the past or the ones you may make in the future. There are two things that are constant in life: 1.*Change* 2.*Mistakes*. They will always happen during our lifetime. The better we accept and learn from them the better our lives become.

Millions of people don't do any thing significant with their lives because of the fear of making mistakes. They don't want to 'mess up' or 'blow it' before others. To save themselves the embarrassment of making a mistake before friends or foes, they accept things as they are and hardly try something new or make much difference with their lives. It's a bigger mistake to try not to do anything new because you don't want to make a mistake. Don't make the big mistake of letting a mistake stop you from making necessary progress in life to enable you create the future you want.

OVERCOME YOUR FEAR OF MAKING MISTAKES
The fear of making mistakes will do three things to you:

1. Limit your potential
You may never know your true capabilities until you take the chance to try something new. We limit our abilities when we avoid the challenge

to confront change. You must get past your fear of making mistakes to unlimit your potentials. If you keep avoiding starting a new business of your own; pursuing a new career, and building new relationships because you are afraid you might make a mistake, you will never know or use all the unique abilities God has blessed you with.

2. Deny you new opportunities

The opportunity to grow; to learn; to be better a person; to make changes, and achieve greatness comes with making some degree of mistakes. You won't be able to make the most of opportunities if you fear making mistakes and will eventually miss out on new ones. George Bernard Shaw, renowned American teacher and speaker rightly said, *"A life spent making mistakes is not only more honourable, but more useful than a life spent doing nothing"*.

3. Increase your chances of making more mistakes

If you spend much time and effort avoiding mistakes (because of your fear of making one) you often end up making more mistakes than you bargained for. The reason is because we become vulnerable to what we are afraid of. Viktor Frankl, Austrian born neurologist and psychiatrist, who survived the concentration camp amid adverse condition and eventually chronicled his experience in a book titled 'Man's search for meaning' said, *"Fear makes come true that which one is afraid of"*.

WHAT TO DO WITH MISTAKES

When things don't go the way you have planned or turn out to be mistakes, don't lose heart or give up trying. Never let a mistake stop you or discourage you from taking further steps to create the future you want. Your next or biggest breakthrough may be the result of a mistake. Here are the best four things you can do with mistakes:

ACCEPT THEM

It's sometimes difficult to accept your own mistakes or the ones made by others, but it's a wise choice to make. Maturity and growth comes with the ability to accept responsibility for the things you do –even if they turned out to be mistakes. Its no use trying to deny or cover up a mistake-it may lead to more complicated ones. Charles Knight (1874-1953), renowned English publisher and author was very correct when he said, *"You need the ability to fail. You cannot innovate unless you are willing to accept some mistakes."*

LEARN FROM THEM

You can gain valuable lessons from the mistakes you have made and those made by others. We can either let mistakes become great teachers or terrible tormentors. Nelson Boswell, famous for his speeches and quotes correctly observed, *"The difference between greatness and mediocrity is often how an individual views a mistake"*.

DON'T REPEAT THEM

I like the prayer once said by Dr William J. Mayo: *"Lord, deliver me from the man who never makes a mistake, and also from the man who makes the same mistake twice."* As a kid I always heard my mum say, "once beaten twice shy". I never knew what that meant until I was grown up. Don't be caught making the same mistake twice or worse still a third time. Learn from your experience the first time and move on. Mistakes were meant to make us smarter than before it happened.

TEACH OTHERS FROM YOUR EXPERIENCE

You can help a lot of people not to make the same mistakes you've made by sharing your experience and the lessons you gained from making your own mistakes with them. They will always appreciate you for helping them. William Arthur Ward (1921-1994), renowned US college administrator and motivator said, *"When we seek to discover the best in others we somehow bring out the best in ourselves."*

"…There is no mistake so great as the mistake of not going on."

-William Blake, British poet, painter and print maker.

DONT LET A MISTAKE STOP YOU FOLLOWUP EXCERISE

Have you ever let a mistake discourage or stop you from achieving the things you desire? If yes in what way did you let such mistakes affect you?

In what specific ways do you think you can overcome your fear of making mistakes?

What lessons have you learnt from the mistakes you have made in the past?

What would you try to achieve in the next 1-3 months if you were not bothered about making mistakes?

How can you teach or help others learn from the mistakes you have made in the past?

8
START SMALL BUT GET BIGGER

"The journey of a thousand miles begins with one step"-Chinese proverb

The journey of a thousand miles truly begins with one step. But I may as well mention the fact that such step must be made in the right direction, and followed up with many more steps for the journey to be completed successfully. It is very important that the steps you take in pursuit of the dreams and future you hold in your heart are made in the right direction. You can take many determined and persistent steps in any given direction but if it is not in the right direction it certainly won't lead you to the right destination.

IT'S YOUR MOVE TO MAKE
If you already know where you want to go (by now you should know or at least have a good idea) then you must know that if you don't make the move to get there, you won't ever be there. You can think, dream, plan and talk about the place you want to be or the future you want to have, but until you take the initiative and make the move that place or future will never be yours. We must walk our talks to have its worth.

START EARLY
There's a huge advantage when you start pursuing your dream early. Compare a football star that started out in his late 20's or mid 30's to a young footballer who started out as a teenager? People like Bill Gates of Microsoft, Richard Branson of Virgin Companies, Sir Alan Sugar of

Amstrad, all started as entrepreneurs in their teenage years. Of course they have all come a long way. Starting early was a major advantage for them.

SET GOALS TO TAKE YOU THERE

You must initiate the steps you will need to take on a daily, weekly, monthly, and annual basis to make happen the things you dream and hope to achieve. You will also need to set many goals (short-term and long-term) to help you pursue and achieve your dreams. Henry Ford, inventor and founder of Ford Motors once said *"Nothing is difficult to achieve if you break it down into many small steps"*. Whatever your dream or goal is, you can break it down into many small steps by setting several small and mid- term goals. Achieving your dreams becomes a lot easier this way. For example if your dream is to start a successful business of your own, your goals could be something like this:

Dream: Start my own business

Goals (short-term)

- Discover a good business idea
- Research/study the idea
- Do a feasibility study
- Develop business idea
- Talk to an expert or somebody in a similar business

Goals (long-term)

- Develop a business plan
- Source for funds (personal saving, Bank, close friends, relatives, etc.)
- Find a good location
- Set a date or period to start

THE BIG THING ABOUT SMALL STEPS

Small steps are powerful. Sometimes, they make the big difference whether or not we accomplish our big goals and dreams. The advantage with taking small steps is that we can make very steady progress which eventually adds up to become significant progress overtime. Having a big or major goal or project can sometimes be overwhelming. But if you break the same big goal into several small steps and part the once overwhelming goal or project looks easier to achieve one step at a time. Remember *"nothing is difficult to achieve if you break it down into many small steps"*

When you take small steps towards any big goal or project you:

    i.   Build momentum
    ii.   Stay motivated
    iii. Maintain focus
    iv. Develop tenacity
    v.   Overcome fear and procrastination
    vi. Stay organized
    vii. Maintain steady progress
    viii.   Have little victories to celebrate to keep you going

Whatever your goals, plans, project or dream may be, find a way of developing small steps you can consistently take until you eventually accomplish your big goal or dream.

TAKE SEVERAL MORE STEPS

Keep the pace of your journey up by taking several more steps. You can only get closer to your destination by taking more steps persistently. To effectively take the many more steps your journey requires, you must be aware of four things: 1.Your resources 2.Your abilities 3.Your opportunities 4.Your obstacles/limitations .You will need to have the first three and must overcome the fourth one to get to your destination.

1. Resources: You will need the means or the 'wherewithal' to get to where you are going and create the future you want. Resources are not only in terms of money (though it's a major part of it). Your time is the biggest resource you have. What you do with it determines the other type of resources you will have. We get paid for what we do with our time. Each time you waste your time or that of someone else, you are wasting away a valuable resource. Every person who achieved something great started out using the first resource God gave them-*time*. Learn to maximise your use of time. If you are planning to start a business learn to save or put cash aside to help you when you start off. If you plan to write books learn how to create the needed time to invest in writing. Whatever your dream is, find creative ways to create the time you need to accomplish your goals.

2. Abilities: You must have the necessary abilities (or develop them) to make the journey (achieve your dreams and the future you desire). Skill and aptitude is an essential part of accomplishing any great dream, plan, goal or purpose. If you don't have the required skill or abilities to achieve the dreams you have, you can start developing them.

3. Opportunities: You will need the right opportunities to achieve your dreams. There is never a lack of opportunities, only a lack of ability to see them. Opportunities will always abound but you must learn to recognize them and make the most of them. Sometimes opportunities show up when you least expect so always be on the look out for one.

4. Obstacles/limitation: Nobody wants them, but we always have them. We must overcome them to achieve our dreams and reach our destination. The path to every great future always has its share of obstacles. But the pride and joy of it all is that you had challenges but you were able to get past them to achieve your dreams.

QUESTIONS THAT NEED ANSWERS

To achieve your dreams there are a lot of questions you will need to ask yourself and provide honest answers to. Some questions are listed below. The purpose is essentially to help evaluate your strengths and weakness, and to know what you need to be able to go the distance. I can't possibly list out all the questions. But within the context of this chapter it's important you ask yourself the following questions:

a) "What resources do I have and will need to achieve my dreams and plans and create the future I want?"
b) "What abilities do I have and would need to achieve my dreams and create the future I want?"
c) "What opportunities do I have and would need to achieve my dreams and create the future I want?"
d) "What obstacles/limitations will I need to overcome to achieve my dreams and create the future I want?"

It will be very helpful if you make a detailed list of the answers after a careful reflection on the questions. This will help you find out what you have from what you need to achieve your dreams and create the future you want. To make this easier for you an exercise is provided below to help you do this.

5 STEPS TO HELP YOU GET THERE

Get a pen ready. You may do some thinking here, but it is meant to help you take the steps you need to achieve your dreams.

STEP 1: Describe in clearly defined terms what your dreams are and the type of future you plan to have (provide as much details as you can).

- .
- .
- .
- .
- .

STEP 2: List (and explain if you can) the resources you think will help you achieve your dreams and plans.

- .
- .
- .
- .
- .

STEP 3: List the abilities that would be necessary to help you achieve your dreams and plans including the ones you already have and may need to develop.

- .
- .
- .
- .
- .

STEP 4: List the opportunities you may need to help you achieve your dreams and plans and enable you create the future you want.

.

.

.

.

STEP 5: List the obstacles or limitations (present ones and the ones you envisage may come up later on) you have to overcome to achieve your dreams.

.

.

.

.

.

If you have taken the time to ask and list the answers to these important questions, it will help you to:

a. Reinforce and internalise a clear picture of what your dream is and the kind of future you want to create for yourself.
b. Know clearly what resources, abilities, and opportunities you already have and the ones you will need to have or develop to achieve your dreams.
c. Know what obstacles or limitations you have to overcome to achieve your dreams and create the future you want.

CONSOLIDATE YOUR STEPS
Like an athlete that is set to win a race, keep developing and applying yourself with every step you take towards your dream and future. Strengthen your steps with discipline and commitment to your goals.

If you have identified a particular resource, ability, or opportunity you need to make your dream happen but don't have presently, concentrate your effort on developing them.

START SMALL BUT GET BIGGER FOLLOWUP EXCERISE

List your 3 short term goals and your 2 long term goals. (if you need more space you may use a seperate sheet)

My short term goals

    1.

    2.

    3.

My long term goals

    1.

    2.

Why are these goals important to you? What would you benefit by achieving these goals?

(People find it easier to succeed and achieve their goals when they see the benefits it will bring to their lives)

Make a list of 5 small steps you can break your goals or dreams into to make it easier for you to make steady progress? (Remember no task or goal is difficult to accomplish if it is broken into several smaller steps)

1.

2.

3.

4.

5.

9
MIND YOUR MIND-SET

"A mind is a terrible thing to waste"

In the early 1920s a Circus group moved to a state in America to stage one of their shows. One of their main events was the display of their very large wild cats in a cage with a very skilled animal handler. One particular evening one of the very large lions escaped from its cage and made its way into the nearby house of an old lady who was just about to have her dinner. She was setting the table for herself and her grandson who was spending the weekend with her when she noticed a large animal walked through her newly cleaned corridor. She dashed to her kitchen and got her large broomstick and headed for the escaped animal. She spotted the large animal at the end of her corridor and attacked it with her broomstick shouting: "you dirty big for nothing donkey, get out of my house. See how much you have messed the floor I just cleaned. Out you go this moment before I break your legs with my broomstick!" The surprised lion ran out the same way it came in. The animal handler and circus organisers who were out looking for the escaped lion soon tracked and caught the large lion and took it back to its cage.

Shortly after this incident a local press quickly arrived the scene and asked the old lady how she managed and where she found the courage to chase such a large animal with only a broomstick from her house. "Oh it was just a silly old donkey who must have missed its way or looking for food" she responded. "No Mrs" the reporter said. "That was a lion you just chased with a broomstick". The old lady fainted in shock. It took a doctor to revive her again. After she regained consciousness she was asked what happened to her. "I didn't have my glasses on and I thought it was a donkey, if I knew it was a lion I would have run out of the house with my grandson!"

IT ALL BEGINS IN THE MIND

It's amazing what people can do when they believe it can be done and it should be done. People have accomplished remarkable feat others once thought was impossible simply because they thought nothing could stop them from achieving their goals. If you would ever accomplish much during your lifetime, you must believe in the possibilities of your dreams and in your ability to achieve the goals you have set for yourself. This is what makes the difference between people who become champions in life and those who become mediocre. The choice is always down to the individual and it always starts in the mind. We win or lose our life's battle in our minds before the reality takes place in real life.

There is so much to learn from the true-life story above about the old lady and the lion she thought was a donkey. As long as she thought the animal was a donkey she believed she could chase it out of her house. In her mind and sub-consciousness she was dealing with a donkey because she saw it that way. She had the strength to chase the animal and could not be paralysed with fear. She was only hit with fear after she dealt with the situation and discovered it was a lion she chased. I am not suggesting you see a lion or face a dangerous situation and pretend its something else in an attempt to deal with it. I am simply relating to how powerful and controlling our mindsets could be in any situation.

A person's mindset determines his/her perception, level of energy, strength of will and character, and ultimately a person's level of success.

Your mindset influences every other area of your life. People try to change their lives without first confronting and changing their mindset. It's like trying to change the structure of a building without first dealing or working on the foundation of the building.

THE MIND-SET SECRET

A mind-set is defined as "A fixed mental attitude or disposition that predetermines a person's responses to and interpretations of situations or the habitual or characteristic mental attitude that determines how you will interpret and respond to situations" (source: answers.com).

To simply state it, your mind-set is your formed thought patterns, opinions, attitude and mentality that forms your habits and behaviours and determines how you respond to situation. It determines what you do and how you make decisions in your daily life. In other words, if I can determine your mind-set I can predict your response to certain situations. I can also determine the end result or outcome if you are faced with certain types of issues, challenges or circumstances. A person's mindset makes a person who he or she is. The Bible in the book of Proverbs states: *"For as he thinks in his heart, so is he." Proverbs 23:7*

Mind-set building or training is used both in the Military, Politics, and Athletics, as well in the Business world. Professionals in these fields know it is the secret to what determines the outcome and results their people face. A person's mind-set could be a powerful or destructive tool. Your mind-set can break or make you. It will be the deciding factor of how you would respond to life challenges and if you would make it through adversity and be a success.

Your mind-set determines your success and your future. You must make every necessary effort to develop and build the right mind-set. You must make every effort also to change the wrong mind-set.

WHAT YOU THINK UPON GROWS

Whatever we think upon grows, takes root, and eventually bears fruit. The mind as earlier stated is a powerful tool. It receives, retains and develops whatever is allowed into it. Nothing goes into a person's mind and comes out the same. This is why we must guard our minds and protect our thoughts. The author of the book of Proverbs understood this fact and clearly advised: *"Carefully guard your thoughts because they are the source of true life."* Proverbs 4:23 (Contemporary English Version).

Your future is connected to your thoughts. Your life will always move in the direction of your most dominant thoughts. Constantly think about bills and paying mortgages and you tend to worry more. On the other hand constantly think about the possibility of having and creating other opportunities of making more money or getting a promotion and you tend to get more excited and become hopeful and creative. The quality of life you would enjoy or experience some years from now is already being shaped by the things you think about the most today. Our thoughts form our actions, which in turn form our future. Thoughts are like seeds. They bear the fruits that eventually crystallize into our future. Charles Reade (1814-1884), an old English dramatist, novelist and journalist said, *"Sow a thought, and you reap an act; Sow an act, and you reap a habit; Sow a habit, and you reap a character; Sow a character, and you reap a destiny."* That statement may have been said nearly 150 years ago but it explains why a lot of people end the way they do. It provides an insight to why some men and women become great and others settle for mediocrity. What you think upon grows. Success starts with a thought. So also does failure.

An outstanding teacher, author and leader, Emmet Fox, shares the following in an article he wrote over 65 years ago

"What you think upon grows. Whatever you allow to occupy your mind you magnify in your life. Whether the subject of your thoughts be good or

bad, the law works and the condition grows. Any subject that you keep out of your mind tends to diminish in your life, because what you do not use atrophies.

The more you think about your indigestion or your rheumatism, the worse it will become. The more you think of yourself as healthy and well, the better will your body be. The more you think about lack, bad times, etc., the worse will your business be; and the more you think of prosperity, abundance, and success, the more of these things will you bring into your life.

The more you think about your grievances or the injustices that you have suffered, the more such trials will you continue to receive; and the more you think of the good fortune you have had, the more good fortune will come to you…What you think upon grows."

DEVELOP AND MAINTAIN THE RIGHT MIND-SET

Having the right mind-set is an important aspect to your succeeding in life and creating the type of future you desire. The right mindset would also help you build a wonderful self-confidence and positive self-image about yourself. It would also affect how you relate with people and what you bring into every relationship in your life. The list is endless to what having the right mindset would do for you, but here are the 5 major areas that are directly affected by our mindset:

1. Health

Your mind-set will dictate the condition of your health. Do you realise our eating habits are a reflection of our value for health? Some people wreck their health by the type of diet they maintain. *You are what you eat* is as true as *what you eat is either killing you or keeping you*. If you have the right mind-set you would naturally respect your body and health and this attitude would be reflected in your eating habits and your living conditions.

2. Wealth

A major difference between the rich and the poor is in their attitude towards issues such as money, work, and time management. The mind-set of the rich view these issues differently from the average person. The rich would rather invest or look for ways to save more money, use their time wisely and be highly productive because of their mind-set. I have also seen lots of people that would rather spend money on things they really don't need, misuse their time and resources and would rather play than work and are poor. Your level of wealth is tied to your mind-set.

3. Relationships

When it comes to relationships our mind-set determines three things: *1. Our perception of people, 2. The type of people we attract to our lives, 3. How we treat the people in our lives.* Our relationships work the way our minds work. If you believe in people it will reflect in the way you relate with them. If you don't trust people it will also reflect in the way you deal with them. Our mind-set forms the basis of our relationships and the quality those relationship will have.

4. Self-image

Our self-image is a direct reflection of the quality of our mind-set. If you have the right mind-set you will naturally have a positive and healthy self-image. A wrong mind-set will either produce a poor self-image or an *over the roof* self-image which is negative as well. Whether people experience inferiority complex or superiority complex, it is simply a direct projection of the type of mind-set they have, *"For as he thinks in his heart, so is he."*

5. Your future

Our mind-set sets the foundation for what our future would become. Whatever your mind-set is today is a definite pointer to the future that lies ahead for you. The reason for this is quite simple: our mind-set determines the way we see life; the way we interpret it; and the way we respond to it. Our thoughts, which are later translated into actions, are the products of our mind-set. Our attitude to life also comes from the type of mentality or mind-set we posses. This is what sets the blocks for a person's future. William James (1842-1910), a pioneering American psychologist and philosopher said, *"The greatest discovery of my generation is that man can alter his life simply by altering his attitude of mind."* Mind your mind-set: it is making or ruining your future!

TO CHANGE YOUR WORLD CHANGE YOUR THOUGHTS

A person is no different from his thoughts. You may have heard this phrase: *"it's not the action that matters; it's the thought that counts"*. Our thoughts are powerful, more potent and powerful than our words or actions because both our words and actions derive their origin from our thoughts. No one can see your thoughts, but they can see your actions and tell your thoughts. The content of your thoughts truly dictates the contents of your life. It is so true what the Bible says in Proverbs: *"Carefully guard your thoughts because they are the source of true life."*

People make desperate attempts to change their lives and circumstances without first addressing the source of the matter-*Their thoughts.* True changes can only occur from *inside out* and not the other way round. Our thoughts are a source of strength or weakness; hope or despair; confidence or self-disbelief; intelligence or stupidity; creativity or the lack of it depending on its contents and how we use it. Interestingly every man or woman is responsible for their own thoughts and the contents of it. Laurence J. Peter, US educator and writer and author of 'Peter's quotation: Ideas of our time', made the following statement:

"Real, constructive mental power lies in the creative thought that shapes your destiny, and your hour-by-hour mental conduct produces power for change in your life. Develop a train of thought on which to ride. The nobility of your life as well as your happiness depends upon the direction in which that train of thought is going."

6 WAYS TO EMPOWER YOUR THOUGHT LIFE

We cannot separate how we think from how we live. The quality of our thoughts will dictate the quality of our life. A person who is weak in thought would be weak in character as well. A person whose thought life is great would express it naturally in his character too. Benjamin Disreali (1804-1884) one of Britain's greatest politician and author rightly said: *"Nurture your mind with great thoughts, for you will never go any higher than you think"*.

A great way to empower your life is to empower your thoughts with positive and productive thoughts. Blaise Pascal, a great French mathematician, physicist and philosopher said, *"Man's greatness lies in his power of thought"*. The following are six proven and effective ways to empower your thought life, which in turn will empower your life:

1. Recognise and deal with negative and unproductive thoughts immediately

The first step is to recognise it when negative and unproductive thoughts come into your mind and learning how to deal with them right then and there. Remember thoughts (good or bad) are like seeds and once settled in the mind they bear fruits that affect every other area of our lives if left unchecked. You must recognise the thoughts that steals your joy; stops your faith; makes you feel worthless; drains your energy; increase self-doubt; makes you feel hopeless; and many other negative and unproductive thoughts that brings out the worst in you. Such thoughts are breeding grounds for a disaster in your life. They take your life in the direction you don't want to go. Thoughts that can mess up your mind can mess up your life. You must recognise such thoughts for what they are and deal with them immediately.

A great way to deal with negative and unproductive thoughts is to refuse to entertain them. Reject them as lies that would mislead and misguide your life. Someone once said *"you can't stop the birds from flying over your head but you can stop them from making a nest on your head"*. Negative and unproductive thoughts are some times like that. You may not be able to stop them from coming to your mind but you certainly can stop them from entering and settling down in your mind and wreck further havoc.

2. Deal with the source of your negative and unproductive thoughts

You would keep fighting the same battles with your thoughts and with your mind every day if you don't deal with the root of the problem. You must find the source of the thoughts you don't want to have and deal with it. Eradicate the source of negative and unproductive thoughts and you can cut off further supplies of similar thoughts.

There are three types of source when it comes to negative and unproductive thoughts: ***people, places, and things.***

People: Your life would be probably better off without the presence of certain people in it. There are certain people with special abilities to bring pain, sorrow, contention and every possible negative feeling to your life. To be honest with you, you don't need such people in your life. Sever such relationships. Yes it may be painful, but it will solve a major source of pain and problem in your life. There are people I don't keep company with anymore because of what they bring with them to my life. Anyone who would cast doubt on your beliefs; cause you to lose your peace; leave you worse than they met you and fill your mind with negative and unproductive thoughts is really not a friend. Refrain from such associations.

Places: Certain places bring out the worst in you. Depending on what your weaknesses are, visiting a particular location would only weaken your thought life. A man battling with lust would be doing himself more harm if he visits a pornographic website or a strip dance club. A lady trying hard to diet but always visiting a fast food restaurant would have a harder time getting the body shape and results she wants. A student having a difficult time making his grades but yet frequenting the clubs and pubs would find himself or herself further away from where they want to be. The places we visit or spend time at will either strengthen or weaken our thought life. They could be a source of negative and unproductive thoughts or the opposite. Chose carefully and wisely where you spend most of your time.

Things: Objects and items could be a source of wrong thought patterns. If you have a possession of something that is a constant source of worry, pain, hopelessness, low self-worth, contention with others, etc, you would have a greater peace of mind and a better thought life if you do without such items in your life. A person whose credit card debt is a constant source of worry and poor self-esteem would likely have less trouble battling with such negative and unproductive thoughts in their hearts if they don't have in their possession credits cards that could lead them into greater debt and financial misery.

It may be a book, CD, film or programme that could be a source of negative and unproductive thoughts. Whatever the source of the negative and unproductive thoughts may be, we must take immediate action to deal with those source or we would be fighting a futile and endless battle trying to stop the thoughts from messing up our lives.

3. Replace negative and unproductive thoughts with positive ones
The next step we need to take to empower our thought life is to replace negative and unproductive thoughts with positive and productive ones. You have identified the thoughts that pull you down and bring out the worst in you and have dealt with them. You have even dealt with the source of the problem. Great! Now is the time to replace those negative and productive thoughts with positive and productive ones. Replace thoughts of fear with confidence; thoughts of disbelief with faith; thoughts of anger with calmness; thoughts of sorrow with joy. Fill your mind with the type of thoughts that can take you to where you want to be. Thoughts that will empower your life and bring about

the fruits and results you want to experience. Danish philosopher and writer, Soren Kierkegaard said: *"Our life always expresses the result of our dominant thoughts"* Choose the thoughts you want to dominate your mind and you will see the results you want manifest itself in your life.

4. Find a source for great and uplifting thoughts

The next step to empower your thought life is to find a good source where you can tap into great and uplifting thoughts that you can fill your mind with. There are loads of resources out there that can inspire you and empower your thought life on a daily bases. Buy and read motivational books. Listen to inspirational speakers. Listen to those who would increase your faith. Connect with those who can increase your self-confidence and belief. Don't let money or time ever come between you and a good book or material. Find a good source for positive and uplifting thoughts and fill your mind with such thoughts always. Ralph Waldo Emerson, one of US greatest poet, essayist and lecturer said: *"A man's what he thinks about all day long."*

I would highly recommend you read the Bible as often as you can. No other book or material in the world can inspire you and fill your heart with hope and faith as much as it does. In addition to being the word of God, it is a collection of some of the greatest stories, events, people, teachings and examples that you can ever have access to in one volume.

5. Share your positive and uplifting thoughts with others

Lastly, in the quest to empower your thought life in order to enjoy the results of an empowered life, you would need to share your positive and uplifting thoughts with others. The benefit of this is two fold:

1. We inspire and encourage others

When we share with others our positive and uplifting thoughts we more often than we realise it lift up the heart of others without even knowing. A lot of people are discouraged and are at the verge of giving up. You might just be the one to make the difference in their lives and give them the needed extra strength to go on. I find that I encourage a lot of people when I share my positive thoughts. It's always a joy for me when someone comes back to tell me they were encouraged by what I said. Ralph Waldo Emerson said, *"To share often and much; to leave the world a little better; to know even one life has breathed easier because you have lived. That is to have succeeded."* Don't hesitate to share your positive and uplifting thoughts-you never know who you might inspire and encourage.

2. You get better and stronger

The second benefit of sharing our positive and uplifting thoughts with others is that we get better and stronger ourselves. Have you noticed that each time you encourage someone or simply solve a problem for others or point them in the right direction you feel good all of a sudden? God designed life to be that way. You would never lack what you give to people. James M. Barrie, Scottish playwright and novelist best remembered today for his fantasy work *Peter Pan,* said: *"Those who bring sunshine to the lives of others cannot keep it from themselves."* Jesus in Luke 6:38 made a profound statement: *"Give away your life; you'll find life given back, but not merely given back—given back with bonus and blessing. Giving, not getting is the way. Generosity begets generosity."* *(The Message Bible)*

Go on and share your positive and uplifting thoughts with people. That way you would empower the life of others and you will experience you won't lack for inspiration to stay empowered.

Practice these truths and principles and you would be amazed at the changes that will take place in your life on a daily basis. Watch your life go from strength to strength and head in the direction you want it to go as your thoughts and life are empowered. The following poem shows us how we can daily empower our lives by empowering our thoughts and creating the changes we desire:

How do I change?
If I feel depressed I will sing.
If I feel sad I will laugh.
If I feel ill I will double my labour.
If I feel fear I will plunge ahead.
If I feel inferior I will wear new garments.
If I feel uncertain I will raise my voice.
If I feel poverty I will think of wealth to come.
If I feel incompetent I will think of past success.
If I feel insignificant I will remember my goals.
Today I will be the master of my emotions.
- Og Mandino

MIND YOUR MIND-SET
FOLLOWUP EXERCISE

How would you best describe the type of mind-set you believe you have?

In what ways can having the wrong mind-set limit you?

In what ways do you think you can improve your mind-set?

What areas of your life would greatly improve you if you had the right mind-set?

1.

2.

3.

4.

What positive and productive thoughts would you like to constantly have?

Exactly what changes and results would you like to see in your life as a result of   thinking more positive and productive thoughts?

10
GO FOR IT!

"All things are possible to him who believes"-The Bible (Mark 9:2)

As this book comes to an end, let it begin a new chapter in your life. I believe you can be more than you are right now. You can achieve your dreams. You have wonderful abilities and gifts that will help you create the future you want. You posses what it takes to make things happen. There is greatness within you waiting to be released and revealed. You have a great future just ahead of you. And all you have to do is *go for it!*

YOU HAVE NO EXCUSES

You don't have any excuses good enough why you can't succeed or achieve your dreams. Someone once said *"People usually have more than a hundred reasons why they can't succeed when all they need is one reason why they can"*. If you try hard enough and apply yourself long enough to your dreams and goals you will find success in the long run. Richard M. Devos declared *"The only thing that stands between a man and what he wants from life is often merely the will to try it and the faith to believe that it is possible."*

JUST DO IT

NIKE, the biggest sports clothing company in the world, has a slogan and a logo I believe explains one of the major reasons for their phenomenal success. It is a simple word that inspires both athletes and non-athletes around the word. This simple slogan is used both in the corporate, academic, political, and business world, as well as in the streets: "*just do it*". It is a simple slogan made popular by *NIKE* that has inspired millions of people to reach for their dreams and achieve it.

Whatever your dreams, goals or aspirations are, "*just do it*".

21 WAYS TO STAY MOTIVATED UNTIL YOU GET THERE

Every one of us needs a little push every now and then to stay motivated and focused until our dreams come to pass and we create the future we want. Progress requires motivation for it to be sustained. Here are 21 ways you can keep yourself motivated until you accomplish your dreams and do the things necessary to create the future we want.

Believe in God
1. Have faith in God-He has all it takes to help you.
2. Believe God loves you enough to want you to succeed.
3. Recognize and accept the fact that He has endowed you with the abilities and talents to achieve your dreams.

Believe in you
4. Recognise your uniqueness. You are unique in every way. Open your eyes and see it.
5. Work on yourself. You can be a hundred times better than you are if you're willing to work it.
6. If you've made mistakes, it doesn't make you a mistake. If you've failed before, it doesn't make you a failure.

Believe in your dreams
7. Remember: *"The future belongs to those who believe in the beauty of their dreams."*
8. You can live your dreams if you try hard enough and work long enough on them.
9. Dare to believe in your dreams. Dreams do come through!

Believe in your abilities

10. Put your gifts and abilities to work. Your gifts and talents often commensurate with your goals and dreams, giving you a real chance to achieve them.

11. People usually end up astonishing themselves with the amazing results they achieve when they put all their abilities to real work.

12. Believe the impossible is possible. "All *things are possible to him who believes*"-The Bible (Mark 9:23)

Maximize your time

13. Have value for time. God gives everyone 8,760 hours every year. How well we use them determines how much we get out of life.

14. Have a sense of urgency when you have something important to do. Your time is your first and best asset through which you create other assets.

15. Invest your time. It will differentiate you from those who just spend it.

Maximize your opportunities

16. Make the most of every opportunity. You will always get a second chance, but you can't be sure of a third one. It's always better to make the most of the first.

17. Learn to recognise opportunities. There is never a lack of opportunity-only the inability to see them on time. Keep your eyes and mind opened. Opportunities abound.

18. Work hard-very hard. Give each chance you get 100% of your best effort. It's the best way to make the most of every opportunity.

Go the extra mile

19. Aspire to always do your best and be the best. Reach for the top. *"There's always room at the top"*-Daniel Webster

20. Only a few people will make the extra effort to go the extra mile-that's why they standout when they do.
21. *"Go the extra mile. It's never crowded"*-Executive speed writer News letter.

Another very Interesting and engaging Book from Daniel Ayeni

30 WAYS TO CHANGE YOUR LIFE IN 30 DAYS
Change the way you think
Change the way you act
Change the way you feel
Change the way you live

This book does not just offer you a challenge to change your life it actually offers you a chance to change your life in 30 different ways in 30 days! Practical facts and principles are presented in this book that would help change the way you think influence the way you act and impact the way you live. Get ready for a change!

About The Author

Daniel Ayeni is a writer, Entrepreneur, and Youth Pastor. He pastors a branch of the New Covenant Church in London. He is the project coordinator of Youth/Young Adults Foundation Network (YFN) and the founder of HUNDREDFOLD EMPOWERMENT, a company dedicated to adding value to the lives of people through personal development and empowerment. He holds a degree in Public Administration. He has a passion to help people fulfill their potentials, achieve their dreams and become the best they can be. He resides with his wife in London, UK.

To recieve a free ebook by the author titled **THE 8 EASY WAYS TO ACCOMPLISH ANY GOAL** visit www.hundredfoldempowerment. co.uk

For more information and resources to inspire and empower your life feel free to visit

www.hundredfold empowerment.co.uk.

www.ingramcontent.com/pod-product-compliance
Lightning Source LLC
Chambersburg PA
CBHW022103170526
45157CB00004B/1465